Career Development Workbook

AN INTERACTIVE GUIDE TO LANDING THE JOB OF YOUR DREAMS.

PART II OF III

CORPORATEMELANINMILLENNIAL.COM

This workbook is dedicated to Kannard for putting up with my hours of stress while researching & writing.

Kay for pushing and motivating me.

Ellis & Ellisha for wanting me to leave a legacy for them.

Mommy & Daddy for putting in me the determination to never give up.

Sincerely yours,

Nikki B
The Millennial Career Coach

Hey There

I'm going to be blunt. Looking for a job SUCKS. It doesn't matter if you're a recent college graduate looking for your first job or have been working 10 years and wanting to make a major career change. It's important that you look for what sets your soul on fire. That's what I'm here for. I'm here to help you find your passion. This workbook was created to be an interactive guide to career freedom.

Career Freedom looks different to everybody. For some, that's being able to wake up everyday and walk into a job that they can work with patients, and for others it's working a job where they can work with their hands. I want to help you learn what type of jobs you should be looking for. I also plan to help you land interviews.

I'm here to take this journey with you. We'll do this together. One step at a time. If you're starting from scratch, I recommend you start from the beginning, otherwise find where you need to go and start from there.

Sincerely yours,

Nikki B
The Millennial Career Coach

Assess Yourself

People are more satisfied with their career when their skill aligns with their job. This is helpful when you know what those skills are.

This section was developed for you to learn your personal skills and interests and what jobs are a good matched based on those skills. Once you are able to identify those things, you will find and keep a job that you are passionate about.

This assessment is based on the MnCareers assessment. This assessment will help you discover your interest and show you how it relates to your interests.

This assessment is a simple 42-statement quiz. It is based on the Holland Interests, which will be explained in further detail after the assessment.

Once the assessment is over, you will find 16 different career clusters. Each cluster will list occupations that align with those clusters.

A few tips to remember:

- Don't Panic if the career choices aren't what you like.
- The goal is to get you to thinking about careers you might enjoy.
- Read each statement on the next page, fill in the items you agree with.

Matching Interests to Occupation

LIKE SKILLS, YOU KNOW WHAT INTERESTS YOU. READ EACH STATEMENT. CHECK EACH ONE THAT INTERESTS YOU.

1. I like to work on cars
2. I like to do puzzles
3. I am good at working independently
4. I like to work in teams
5. I am an ambitious person, I set goals for myself
6. I like to organize things, (files, desks/offices)
7. I like to build things
8. I like to read about art and music
9. I like to have clear instructions to follow
10. I like to try to influence or persuade people
11. I like to do experiments
12. I like to teach or train people
13. I like trying to help people solve their problems
14. I like to take care of animals
15. I wouldn't mind working 8 hours per day in an office
16. I like selling things
17. I enjoy creative writing
18. I enjoy science
19. I am quick to take on new responsibilities
20. I am interested in healing people
21. I enjoy trying to figure how things work

RIASEC

Matching Interests to Occupation

LIKE SKILLS, YOU KNOW WHAT INTERESTS YOU. READ EACH STATEMENT. CHECK EACH ONE THAT INTERESTS YOU.

22. I like putting things together or assembling things
23. I am a creative person
24. I pay attention to details
25. I like to do filing or typing
26. I like to analyze things (problems/ situations)
27. I like to play instruments or sing
28. I enjoy learning about other cultures
29. I would like to start my own business
30. I like to cook
31. I like acting in plays
32. I am a practical person
33. I like working with numbers or charts
34. I like to get into discussions about issues
35. I am good at keeping records of my work
36. I like to lead
37. I like working outdoors
38. I would like to work in an office
39. I'm good at math
40. I like helping people
41. I like to draw
42. I like to give speeches

R I A S E C

Let's Break it Down

1. Add all of the columns at the bottom of the chart above. Write down the number of the filled circles for each letter. Write down the number of filled circles for each letter here.

   R = Realistic   Total:
   I = Investigative   Total:
   A = Artistic   Total:
   S = Social   Total:
   E = Enterprising   Total:
   C = Conventional   Total:

2. Take the three letters with the highest scores and record them under "My Interest Code"

   ## MY INTEREST CODE

   _____   _____   _____

3. Turn the page to see what it means.

Results of the RIASEC Test

R = Realistic people are DOERS.

You are practical, reserved, curious, and persistent. You are good at problem solving and working with your hands. You like being outdoors and prefer electronics, mechanics, engineering, farming, and other hands on activities.

A = Artistic people are CREATORS

You are intuitive, sensitive, and imaginative. You hate consistency. You like to be able to work in situations where you can be creative and come up with new ideas. You enjoy performing or creating art. You are often found at museums or concerts and plays. You enjoy fashion, creative writing, drawing, or creating new things n a variety of new settings.

E = Enterprising people are PERSUADERS

You are enthusiastic, assertive, adventurous, and talkative. You need to start new projects and like to make decisions that affect others. You like to work with other people and prefer to be in positions of leadership. You like to influence and persuade. You are good at selling things, promoting things, and managing people. You'd be a great business owner or politician.

I = Investigative people are THINKERS

You are curious, observant, and analytical. You'd prefer to work alone instead of on a team. You're good at math, science, and analyzing data. You like solving puzzles and figuring out hard problems. You're comfortable reading and investigating, or even figuring out computer equipment.

S = Social people are HELPERS

You are friendly, cooperative, responsible, and empathetic. You like to work directly with people instead of things. You like working on teams. YOu love teaching and counseling. You may enjoy team sports. You'd be a good public speaker or trainer. You like to work with children, people with special needs, elderly, or diverse population.

C = Conventional people are ORGANIZERS

You are respectful, orderly, persistent, and practical. You like working with numbers and are good at following instructions. You like being structured and setting goals and deadlines. You are detailed and like working with data. You are great at making sure things work efficiently and effectively.

Use the information above to determine what fields you could be interested in. https://www.rivier.edu/career-development/career-planning/self-assessment-2/occupations-list-by-holland-code/ lists every option along with what degree is needed for that career.

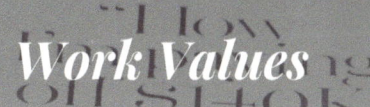

Work Values

A value is something that is important to you.

Look through the list and circle the values important to you. As you set your job goals, keep these in mind, especially the circled ones. Understanding these values help you find a job that's a good fit for you.

JOB SATISFACTION

- Enjoy and feel good about the work that I do
- Be able to direct and supervise others
- Challenging and interesting work
- My company has a good reputation
- Able to use skills in a positive way
- Opportunities for development
- Access to skills, training, and tools

MONEY

- Salary
- Advancement
- Benefits (sick leave, vacation, etc)
- Location of the Job
- Maternity/Paternity Leave

WORK ENVIORNMENT

- Safe work conditions
- Clean work conditions
- Quiet work area
- Ability to work from home
- Culturally diverse

SUPERVISION STYLE

- A lot of supervision
- Some supervision
- Little supervision
- Have a supportive and fair supervisor

MY TOP 3 VALUES

ASSESS YOURSELF: REVIEW

Now you should have a better idea of what your goals and interests are. Think about what you learned as you complete this section.

WHAT DID YOU LEARN ABOUT YOURSELF AND YOUR ABILITIES BY TAKING THE ASSESSMENT?

HOW DO YOU PLAN TO USE THE INFORMATION YOU LEARNED IN THIS SECTION?

Create a Plan

Do you really know what you want in a job and how to get there? This section is all about focuses on creating plans and setting the goals that will land you not just any job, but your dream job.

Goals aren't about talking the talk. They're about walking the walk. The secret to career success is about making an actual plan to getting the stuff done, and that's what this section is all about.

This is made to help get you moving and get you motivated. Most people know that setting goals sounds good in theory, but don't know how to put it into action.

Successful goals have to be 5 things. They have to be SMART. SMART means they must be Specific, Measureable, Achievable, Realistic, and Timely.

This section will also focus on planning. I want you to know what you're looking for in a career. We can think about these things all day long but seeing it in black and white can really make a difference in how we go about our job search.

Let's get started.

Career Planning Worksheet

Date available for work:
Three careers I would start right away:
1.
2.
3.
Minimum (reasonable) Salary to make me happy to go to work each day: $
Benefits I must have:
☐ Health Insurance
☐ Paid Time Off
☐ Life Insurance
☐ Working from Home
☐ Flexible Working Hours

Do you have any physical limitations?

Job Search Schedule

You should have a plan for your job search. There should not be a weekday you should NOT be doing something related to job searching when unemployed. Include some of the following items when thinking of your job search. It's not simply "applying for jobs everyday."

- Contact your local Goodwill
- Utilize LinkedIn (I offer LinkedIn services)
- Research employers you are interested in
- Network
- Update your resume (I do that too!(
- Write your cover lever
- Track application status and reach out to any that are in limbo
- Attend a job fair
- Join local career Facebook groups
- Fil out at least 5 applications a week
- Follow-up with employers after interviews
- Practice interview questions
- Reach out to your network
- Join professional affiliations for your career group

Goals that are written down and shared are more likely to be completed. Have a friend HOLD YOU ACCOUNTABLE in your job search. If you're being honest with yourself about the tasks you are taking on a daily basis, you will begin to see results sooner.

CREATE A PLAN: REVIEW

You should now have a calendar of what you will accomplish on a daily basis Think about what you learned as you complete this section.

WHAT WILL YOU BE COMPLETING DURING YOUR FIRST WEEK?

HOW DO YOU PLAN TO USE THE INFORMATION YOU LEARNED IN THIS SECTION?

Land the Job

We're finally getting down to business! This section is all about getting what you really bought this workbook for. It's about improving the skills you already have or learning new ones.

This section will teach out about some tools every job seeker should have in their pocket. It will focus on what to bring to interviews, body language, body language, and more.

This section is designed to help you LAND THE JOB.

This section is all about some tips and tricks to land the job. It's focused on the highest level skills that are necessary to do well during the interview stage and pre-interview stage.

Part III of III will go into the weeds of how to land the job.

Let's get started.

References - Quiz

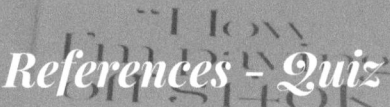

Circle T for true if you think that this person is a good employment reference. Circle F for false if you don't think they would be.

1. A supervisor from a job you were employed at for 5 months. **T or F**

2. One of your former high school or college teachers. **T or F**

3. Your grandmother. **T or F**

4. A supervisor from your job you worked at for 16 months. **T or F**

5. A manager who fired you 3 months ago. **T or F**

6. Your parole officer. **T or F**

7. Your auntie's husband's great uncle. **T or F**

8. Your former coworker. **T or F**

9. Your 1st grade teacher. **T or F**

10. Your pastor or religious leader. **T or F**

11. The head of the company your volunteer with. **T or F**

12. Your social worker. **T or F**

13. Your Narcotics Anonymous sponsor. **T or F**

14. Your elderly neighbor whose lawn you mow. **T or F**

References - Quiz Answers

1. False. In order for a reference to be a qualified reference, they should know you at least a year, preferably more.

2. True. A good reference should be able to talk about your work habits and an old teacher can do that.

3. False. Your grandmother knows you well, but she's subjective. It's best to avoid using family members.

4. True. A supervisor who managed you for a long time is able to be objective about your work.

5. False. A manager who fired you is probably going to give you a bad reference. It's best to avoid that possibility.

6. True and False. Does your P.O like you?!

7. False. I'm sure you guy's aren't close enough to discuss your moral character.

8. True. It is better to have a reference in a leadership position, however a coworker can discuss your work habit, skills, and moral character.

9. False. They don't know who you have grown to be.

10. False. Avoid references that can be controversial.

11. True. A volunteer leader can discuss work skills, duties, and moral character.

12. False. Avoid references that may create concern for your employer.

13. False. Avoid references that may create concern for your employer.

14. True. Although you should definitely give more professional candidates they can verify your moral character and work ethic.

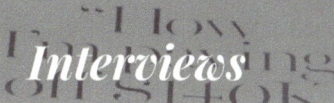

Interviews

Interview etiquette is something many don't live by today. In order to be successful in an interview you must prepare for them beforehand. Piss poor preparation results in piss poor performance is something many athletes have heard before, but the same can be said when it comes to interviewing.

Interviewing can be stressful. This guide allows you to put all of the details you need to remember in one. Print out a copy for every interview and you have it ready to go.

TO-DO:

- [ ] Lay out outfit
- [ ] Pack bag: resume, charget, mints, deodorant, wallet, notepad, pen, portfolio
- [ ] Check interview location and contact information

    Address

- [ ] Review interview questions
- [ ] Fill out your cheat sheet (next page)
- [ ] Research my interviewers on LinkedIn
- [ ] Plan breakfast

Interview Cheat Sheet

Fill this out & take a copy with you to each interview.

DATE:

TIME:

LOCATION:

COMPANY:

POSITION

INFO ABOUT THE COMPANY (ACCOMPLISHMENTS, CULTURE, ETC)

ELEVATOR PITCH: (WHAT YOU'VE DONE IN THE PAST, WHAT YOU'RE DOING NOW. DO NOT REITERATE YOUR RESUME)

WHY THIS POSITION EXCITES ME:

QUESTIONS I'M GOING TO ASK THE INTERVIEWER:

Interview - Quiz

Interview etiquette is something many don't live by today. Let's see how much you know about what to wear and what to bring to an interview.

1) On the day of my interview I should wear:
a. Jean shorts
b. Khaki pants
c. My shortest skirt

2) On the day of my interview I should:
a. Shower, brush my teeth, put on deodorant, and comb my hair
b. Roll out of bed and catch a bus to the interview
c. Dye hair orange, paint my nails to match hair, put on chain, and show off tattoos

3) I should bring to turn in my job application and to my interview:
a. My girlfriend and three kids
b. Copies of my resume, references, pen, notebook, and ID
c. Cigarettes and cell phone

4) I should arrive at my interview:
a. Right when it is supposed to start
b. 15 minutes late. It is good to be fashionably late
c. 10-15 minutes before it starts

5) On the day of my interview, I should wear:
a. Tennis shoes
b. Dress shoes
c. Sandals

6) After the interview, I should:
a. Contact the employer immediately to see if s/he has made a decision yet
b. Write a thank you note or email including any follow-up questions I have
c. Contact the employer multiple times per day, every day, until s/he has decided

7) During my interview, I should:
a. Answer my cell phone when it rings
b. Keep my hat on and use slang and curse words
c. Give clear answers. Sit up straight. Make eye contact with my interviewer

Correct answers: 1. B, 2. A, 3. B, 4. C, 5. B, 6. B, 7. C

Tell Me About Yourself Checklist

This worksheet was created to answer the dreaded question.... tell me about yourself. This is your elevator pitch. These are the things you want your interviewer to remember. Where many people fail in terms of this question is that they simply reiterate their resume. They know your resume already, they want to know about YOU. Answer some of these questions to see how you can tell your future employer about yourself.

LIST YOUR 3 BEST QUALITIES AND A REAL LIFE EXAMPLE OF A TIME YOU DEMONSTRATED EACH QUALITY.

1.

2.

3.

WHAT IS YOUR BIGGEST ACHIEVEMENT SO FAR? WHY?

1.

WHAT'S AN OBSTACLE YOU OVERCAME? WHAT DID YOU LEARN?

2.

WHAT'S SOMETHING YOU'RE PASSIONATE ABOUT WORK-RELATED?

3.

Tell Me About Yourself Checklist

Pull it all together!

You've got everything you need now. Reread all of your answers. Look at the most interesting ones that you wrote, and summarize those into a short story.

Start with these

"People describe me as _____, _____, and _____. (Use the 3 best qualities.).

OR

"I love to _____ (something you're passionate about that deals with the job you're applying for." Then explain what you do to stay current in the business and how you continue to improve your skills. Describe what your goals are in relation to your passion. For example, if your passion is working with people perhaps you're working your way through Toasmasters Pathways program.

Practice

Practice with a friend, or with me as your career coach during a mock interview. You'll be better prepared during your interview and you will feel more comfortable. My next workbook with delve into over 50 different interview questions and how to answer them. Go forth and ROCK your next interview!!

I'm always a message away to help.

Thank You...

My hope for you is that part II of this workbook has been able to give you some sense of career direction. Even if one section was able to help you, please let me know. If there is anything in particular you'd like to see in the final workbook, shoot me an email.

I do this because of you. Best of luck in your career search, change, or career journey!

Warmly

Nikki

CORPORATEMELANINMILLENNIAL.COM

Land Your Dream Career!

NOTES

NOTES

www.ingramcontent.com/pod-product-compliance
Lightning Source LLC
Chambersburg PA
CBHW041320180526
45172CB00004B/1165